Dirty Talk

The Essential Guide For Couples, Packed With Powerful Kama Sutra And Tantric Sex Positions And Transform Your Sexual Life And Learn How To Drive Your Partner Absolutely Wild By Using Dirty Talk

Tomislav Kramer

TABLE OF CONTENT

Introduction 1

Creating Exchanges That Will Eventually Result In Connections 8

Sexuality Education For Young People 20

Important Dos And Don'ts Regarding Conversations In The Dirt 24

Engage Her In Fantasy Roleplaying 37

Taking Turns At Happiness And Setting Limits 41

Indicator Sexual Gps 1 – Connect To Your Satellite: 47

Acknowledging One's Physical Maturity While Taking Ownership Of One's Body 70

You Are The Most Important Thing In Her Life. 76

You're In The Friendzone If... These Texts Keep Coming Up 90

The Technique Of Starting A Conversation Without Fear Of Being Rejected 99

Having A Conversation About Gender Identity 104

The Things That Men Want From Women 110

What Contributes To A Decline In Attractiveness? 115

How To Get Your Exciting Texts Started In A Snappy Manner 133

Strategies For Creating Sexual Tension Via Text Message With A Woman 137

Introduction

To seduce another person is possible in a number of different methods, especially in the technologically advanced society of today. So now you know how to have phone sex if that's something you've ever been curious about.

Because the vast majority of people find having sex over the phone to be more embarrassing than sexy, a lot of people have inquired how it can be done.

Nevertheless, there are a few people for whom phone sex is second nature.

If you are familiar with the small sensuous elements that differentiate a sexual discussion from an uncomfortable one, then mastering the art of exciting your partner over the phone is not a difficult task at all. The reality is that you can easily become an expert in this area.

To make this perfectly clear, sex over the phone is almost never planned in advance. It seems to occur everytime either of you makes an incorrect remark while you are on the phone. It would be the sexiest thing you could do with each other from a distance if you were both able to talk about how horny you were feeling without spoiling the mood.

What exactly is meant by the term "phone sex"?

Phone sex can also be done through the use of aural sex. On the other hand, aural sex refers to a form of sexual stimulation in which you become turned on by listening to something that excites you sexually rather than engaging in sexual activity directly.

Nearly every couple has tried at least one type of sexual activity over the phone at some point, particularly in the beginning of a sexual relationship.

Have you ever picked up the phone to talk to your significant other about how much you miss them, especially when you were in the mood to get horny? If you've ever engaged in phone sex, consider yourself a veteran of the practice.

However, the tone of your voice and the words that you choose to say after that line will determine whether or not you are having a sexual or sexually suggestive conversation.

If the idea of having phone sex with your spouse makes you feel uncomfortable because it sounds inappropriate, you should begin by engaging in filthy texting with them. Just as things start to get heated up, give your lover a call and carry on the discussion over the phone instead.

The history of phone sex goes back quite a ways.

Even if you probably weren't exposed to this kind of instruction in school, let's take a quick detour through history before we get into the specifics of how to have sex over the phone! You probably wished that you had, but that's a different story altogether.

In any event, the sex trade has been around for as long as there have been humans. Since the beginning of time, people have been paying for sex with prostitutes. However, we are not going to be discussing that kind of sex over the phone at all. We are referring to the kind of conversation that one may have with a friend. On the other hand, the development of the sexual services sector in relation to contemporary forms of sex over the phone is a fascinating topic.

It is said that Gloria Leonard was the first person to make money in the adult entertainment industry by calling 900 numbers. She updated her readers with a recording of her own voice that she had recorded and included in the following issue of her magazine. There is no question that she did it in a sexually suggestive and alluring manner.

For a considerable amount of time, the phone sex industry had a good amount of popularity. Even though it isn't *as much* as it used to be, that doesn't mean that it hasn't had a substantial impact on people's personal phone sex activities.

The good news is that if you have phone sex with someone you already know, you won't have to worry about having to pay for it! Those outdated phone sex lines could end up being extremely pricey. You definitely deserve praise for your frugal nature and for going it alone.

Why would you want to engage in phone sex when you could simply engage in sexual activity?

We humans like having a change of pace every once in a while. After a few years of having sex in the same missionary position without conversing dirty or fantasizing in bed, sex may begin to feel like a duty that is best avoided after a certain amount of time has passed.

In the same vein, why is making out in public or touching each other in a car more pleasant than just making out in private?

This is due to the fact that our thoughts are continuously wanting new sexual experiences that have the potential to heighten arousal.

If you and your partner aren't in the same room at the same time, having sex over the phone can provide you the much-needed variety and amplified sensation of pleasure that you're looking for.

If you and your spouse are in a long-distance relationship, engaging in sexual activity over the phone can help keep you both sexually satisfied while also reducing the likelihood that one of you will cheat on the other.

Creating Exchanges That Will Eventually Result In Connections

The art of being able to carry on a conversation is quickly becoming extinct. It is because of the prevalence of sound bites in culture as well as social media that this is the case. When forced to engage in conversation with another person, everyone has an uncomfortable feeling similar to that of a deer caught in headlights at first. And there is a hurry in society to normalize and cater to this anxiety as quickly as possible. You may have noticed that many kiosks are now taking the place of people. It is not simply due to the fact that the kiosk is less expensive than a real person. Another reason is that people in today's society are not very good at being social.

In the beginning of the conversation, in particular, all of us experience this feeling of inner uneasiness, even though there is no obvious cause for us to feel it. This is primarily due to the fact that you are unable to know what the other person is thinking about you. And when the other person is a 9 or a 10, you automatically think that they are looking down on you because you regard them to be so much more attractive and precious than you are. In their hearts, many guys have the idea that the woman they are chatting to is beneath them, much less deserving of anything more.

After a certain point in the conversation, you will start to pick up on hints that may indicate if she has positive or negative thoughts about you. It's possible that you won't receive anything even somewhat similar to that for a very long time. This is the primary factor that inhibits the majority of guys from ever even trying.

You should, however, make the assumption that she is intrigued, attracted, and aroused by you right from the bat in order to eliminate the need to worry about this issue in the first place. If you truly believe this, then you will behave as though it were the case. And when you act as though it is true, she will even begin to think and feel the same way about it as she does when you do. Your actions will serve as a model for hers.

Your ability to converse, which you may have forgotten, can be rediscovered if you make and believe this assumption. It will enable you to effortlessly go from one topic to another without any difficulty. to maintain a natural flow, to inquire into larger depths of another person's personal life and particular worries, and then to bring it back around to lighthearted laughter. In both directions.Skipping over small conversation with relative ease. Also, let's not forget to elicit feelings in the audience.

You aren't merely someone who talks. You move quickly past the stage of superficially getting to know one another and establish a profound and meaningful connection that is mutually beneficial to all parties concerned.

It is far simpler to say than it is to actually carry through. But the payoff was substantial. It will provide you access to opportunities that other abilities simply cannot provide. This is a skill that may be put to use in any situation.

When people believe they have reached a point where they are competent at something, they stop working to improve it. Consider this:

when was the last time you took the time to work on improving the way you drive your car? We have a tendency to compare conversation to riding a bike, in the sense that if you master the fundamentals, you have mastered the skill completely and there is nothing else to learn. But the fact of the matter is that conversation is a talent that can be constantly honed and improved upon. Nearly never cease striving for perfection.

On the other hand, the more you do something and are exposed to it, the more natural it will feel to you. It seems less like a task or a talent that you need to work on developing and more like something that is simply a part of enjoying your life.

Conversational skill training is often neglected by many people since it requires mastery of such a diverse range of subskills. while there are a lot of moving parts to a talent, it's quite simple for individuals to feel scared or overpowered by it while they're trying to learn it for the first time. To be an excellent conversationalist, you need to be able to control your feelings, choice of words, expressions, voice tone, body language, readings of other people's emotions, keeping the discussion fruitful, and removing humiliation from others when they make a mistake by saying something awkward.

This seems like a lot more than it should be. There are way too many moving pieces in this.

However, when you are able to do this, you will possess a superpower. Simply put, people enjoy conversing with you. You rapidly become acquainted with the folks around you. You develop meaningful bonds quite quickly. You are also more likely to receive what it is that you want. You have the ability to negotiate deals. Convince fresh people to your side. Use your charm to get past the obstinate club bouncers.

If there was one thing that functioned as the key to unlocking all of this potential goodness and making it possible to multitask in a way that was manageable and easy, it would be this: having a real interest in other people. This was the most important takeaway I got from reading How to Win Friends and Influence People by Dale Carnegie.

Despite the fact that other individuals might be interesting, we frequently find that we have very little interest in them. However, this is mainly due to the fact that the first impression that we receive of other individuals is frequently erroneous. For the sake of simplicity, our minds have a tendency to group people together into similar categories. A lot of the time, we wrongly believe that our categorization represents the totality of who they are. This is simply due to the fact that you have not yet developed the talent of getting to know individuals on a deeper level.

It's very similar to the game of baseball. Once you have mastered the game, participating in it may be a lot of fun, despite the fact that it is terribly dull to watch. However, before you get skilled at it, the art of conversation is more comparable to the sport of soccer. Extremely uninteresting to watch, and quite taxing on the body to participate in.

However, if you have a real interest in the people around you, this obstacle will be much easier to overcome. You don't even need to enjoy making small chat or any of the more technical aspects of conversing in order to achieve this. You simply need to enjoy the company of other people. You need to have a strong interest in what makes people tick and what motivates them to do what they do, just as David Shore, the creator and producer of the television show House M.D. You want to be in a similar position as he was.

What's Wrong With Programs That Encourage Moderation Before Marriage?

Many students participate in programs that encourage abstinence until marriage in lieu of or in addition to programs that are more comprehensive.

The following programs:

Make it clear to young people that the only moral choice they can make is to forgo a traditional marriage.

Only bring up birth control in regard to its high rate of ineffectiveness.

The needs of LGBTQ adolescents should be ignored in favor of the heterosexual youth population.

They frequently promote archaic notions of gender roles, such as encouraging "modesty" in all females while depicting guys as sexual beings.

It was discovered to have inaccurate information.

They do not have the backing of the majority of people in the United States. It has been demonstrated that the only method that is successful in helping young people delay their first sexual encounter is an abstinence-only program.

Those who engage in sexual activity, on the other hand, put themselves in a precarious position when knowledge regarding methods of birth control is kept secret. Studies have shown that nearly everyone will use some kind of contraception at some time in their lives, and that providing information about available methods of birth control does neither hasten the commencement of sexual activity or increase the amount of sexual activity that takes place. Now, after thirty years of research in the field of public health, it is abundantly obvious that comprehensive sexual education can help young people delay sexual beginning while also assisting them in protecting themselves when participating in sexual activity. We want young people to behave responsibly when making decisions regarding their sexual health, and this means that society has a responsibility to provide them with accurate, age-appropriate, and comprehensive sexual health education; access to pregnancy and sexually transmitted infection prevention services; and resources that will help them live healthy lives. Every single rising young star requires all-encompassing sexual health education as well as sexual health care. There is a possibility that adolescents who are at a disproportionate risk of sexual inequity require focused therapies that are specifically geared to enhance self-efficacy and agency. Additionally, administrators and other policymakers need to acknowledge the fact that structural determinants, sociocultural factors, and cultural norms have been shown to have a powerful impact on adolescent sexual health and need to be addressed in order to truly address sexual health inequality that is fueled by social inequality.

Sexuality Education For Young People

Why it's Important for Parents to Talk to Their Children About Sexuality. If parents do not teach their children about sex and sexuality, the youngsters will learn about these topics somewhere else, and the opportunity to instill family values could be missed.

The Essentials

When your kid is still young, it's important to start having conversations with them about sexuality, and you should keep those conversations going as they become older. • At a far younger age than many parents anticipate, their children will be exposed to knowledge about sexuality from a variety of sources including school, friends, and the media.

Parents should not put their trust in the public school system to educate their children about sexuality. If you know that the school where your child attends teaches sexual education, you should talk to them about what they have learned and go over it with them.

Promiscuity is not caused by receiving sexual education. It's a good idea to get a head start on keeping notes of approximate interactions that are appropriate for the child's developmental stage.

After gaining knowledge about the body, the next natural step is to be curious about how people interact with one another. Children benefit from participating in sexual education because it teaches them about the body and enables them to feel more confident about themselves and their own bodies. Younger youngsters are more fascinated by the prospect of becoming pregnant and giving birth than they are by the act of sexual activity itself. In addition to this, beginning an open line of communication with your child includes having a conversation about interaction. Early on, real, and open communication between parents and children can be very important, particularly when your child is becoming a teenager in their own right. If open communication is practiced on a daily basis, children are significantly more likely to discuss with their parents about nearly all of the many challenges that come with adolescence. These challenges can include anxiety, depression, relationships, and the use of drugs and alcohol, in addition to sexual concerns. The best way to educate a child about appropriate sexual conduct is to start talking to them about it when they are young and to continue doing so as they get older. If it is at all possible for the parents to avoid having a significant conversation with their child after the child has reached the age of adolescent (when the child may already have obtained records and erroneous information from their peers), then they should do so. The easiest way to have these discussions is when they are prompted by a real experience, such as coming into contact with a pregnant woman or a newborn child. It is possible for parents to guarantee that their children are receiving accurate information on intercourse by having a conversation with their children about the topic. The parents are a child's initial and most reliable source of information regarding interactions. Young people who have access to accurate records have an advantage when it comes to avoiding explosive behavior as they mature.

Important Dos And Don'ts Regarding Conversations In The Dirt

We are able to obtain some extremely crucial information that is not available anywhere else thanks to women's publications and blogs. We present concepts and points of view that enable people to comprehend the issues they face and develop strategies to deal with or satisfy those issues. Many women still feel embarrassment when they experiment with using vulgar language for the first time.

It is likely that your partner has the same dirty thoughts about language that you do, but someone should still take the initiative to start the conversation. To really let go and enjoy yourself in the bedroom, all you really need are some pointers. You won't find the dirty conversation beneficial if you follow these few dos, so let's get to it.

The Important Things to Remember:Give him an idea of the scale of it. Men are the perfect complement to being suckers. Get him feeling wonderful about his accomplishments, his skills, and his body. This should make sense in conjunction with what he should be doing. You need to tell him what to do, how to fulfillyou, and how to make you feel more dirty talk by letting him know what you want.

Before getting into bed, you should work on building your sexual confidence just as you would with any other aspect of your life. Wordplay, pre-play courting, and even sex are all fair game in this context. One positive aspect is that it establishes both the pace and the mood for what is to come.

Telling your guy how you feel is the most effective technique to engage in dirty talk since it allows the conversation to flow more organically. It's a good idea to start out by letting him know how amazing you feel on the inside.

The response to this kind of dirty conversation could be anything as simple as "Yes!", but it could also be something like "I feel so good" or "yes, I like it, I really love it." However, folly is directly proportional to how honest and uninhibited both you and your husband are. Although it takes time to create trust, you will eventually be able to.

Do not overdo it or make an excessive effort. Take care not to overdo it. It's possible that what you saw on porn stars is true, but if you start yelling all of the filthy phrases that you can think of, you'll ruin the vibe for everyone. It is preferable to keep things light and honest rather than to completely wreck the mood.

If it isn't helping you, there's no use in continuing to do it. Before engaging in pre-playing, sexing and word playing are both quite important here. You will be able to tell whether or not your partner is going along with the plan or fighting it.

To have a better grasp on the meaning of "dirty talk," you might find it helpful to consult a manual or an eBook that provides an in-depth explanation of the topic. Carry out some research in order to locate the most helpful training handbook, and use it as a guide beginning with the fundamentals of foul language.

Everyone has never before engaged in filthy conversation while having sexual relations. Very few of us actually do it, despite the fact that the vast majority of us want to, even if only in our fantasies.

We are all aware that having sex can be an exciting experience; yet, if couples do not push themselves to do new things, the experience can become repetitive and boring. Your sexual life will improve as a result of dirty conversation; nevertheless, there are certain essential things you can do and certain things you don't have to do in order to make the most out of your experience.

It's possible that your friend wants to use the same foul language as you do, but you won't be able to reignite the flame until you make an effort. You need to ease into it; you can't just start screaming the most inappropriate things that come to mind right away.

It is ideal to begin by subtly whispering in the ears of your partner, letting them know what you want them to do or say, and observing how they react to your instruction. You are going to interpret it as a sign to either say something or act on it. It is normal for the first time to be a little difficult, but one of you will step up and take the initiative to roll the ball.

Think about the possibility of engaging in sleazy conversation for a few months as you get to know your partner and the kinds of things they are interested in.

For the third month of our marriage, I proposed to my partner that I speak to him in a vulgar manner, and to my surprise, he was just the kind of person who would enjoy that type of stuff. Do not begin engaging in vulgar conversation on the first night because it has the potential to turn off some people and could be seen as blatantly disrespectful.

It takes a lot of practice to become an expert nasty talker. Experience is the only way to learn what your spouse wants to hear, what words or phrases turn him or her off, and what physical activities should follow what you say to each other when you are together.

It is essential to keep in mind that engaging in sleazy conversation during sexual activity is not for everyone. My friend Lisa, who was a Christian and very reserved, once told me that she tried to dirty speak in bed with her husband in order to spice things up but unfortunately, that had the opposite effect and caused him to immediately lose his erection. She told me this story because she wanted to spice things up but she was a Christian and very reserved.

Not only did it result in an uncomfortable circumstance, but it also caused a needless pejorative label to be applied to it as a result of what it caused. The point being made here is that you need to be familiar with the company you keep in order to know with absolute certainty whether or not you are engaging in dirty conversation.

It's impossible for anything negative to come from using foul language, right? Not true! In the context of sexual interactions, "dirty talk" does not refer to the act of spitting a string of foul or disgusting phrases in rapid succession, as was indicated earlier. It is not so much the words themselves that are important as how and when they are said. You want to avoid coming off as a tat; the ramblings in porn movies are not the same thing as talking nasty. Erotic discourse, on the other hand, when done correctly, can actually increase the amount of love and affection you share with your spouse. Even if you are only having a one-night stand or are in a casual relationship, you may still improve your sexual experience by using dirty talk in the right way.

Let's take a moment to run through a few of the potential problems that can arise from using foul language.

The celebration of birthdays and the arranging by parents of cultural outings for groups of children to places like the movie, circus, or museum are both excellent avenues for dialogue between males and females of both sexes. At this point, you need to focus the attention of the boys on how they should act towards the females in their lives. Girls, on the other hand, need to demonstrate that they are capable of behaving in a humble and unpretentious manner in order to teach boys and earn their respect and attention.

A young boy who is old enough to be in elementary school should be aware that he should step aside to let a female enter the classroom, school, or movie theater first, that he should give up his seat on the bus, and that he should hand up his coat. There are, nevertheless, some parents who continue to contend, "What is the demand for a child? When he is older, he will know how to act when he is around a girl!

When boys are at school, they are exposed to environments that are conducive to the development of behaviors that are traditionally associated with men.

It is essential to instill in young boys the attributes of a strong will, which includes the capacity to tame their ardor, wants, and instincts, and this education must begin at an early age. Even if it goes against their inclination, children need to learn to put the needs of others before their own. It is essential to begin developing one's capacity for self-control well before the emergence of sexual feelings. Because of this, a child in the first grade needs to learn how to exercise self-control. He needs to have the awareness to know that some of his desires won't be fulfilled and that he must let go of those impulses. It is essential to instill in the youngster the value of giving to others rather than taking from them and finding fulfillment in doing so. V. A. Sukhomlinsky believed that it was necessary to begin teaching students, beginning in the first grade, the ability to perceive the state of mind of another person, such as his delight, anxiety, or grief, and to respond to all of this with thoughts, acts, and deeds. He felt this to be necessary from the beginning of the educational process. It is important for the youngster to have the ability to "read" the emotions, experiences, pleasures, and sufferings of other people.

Misha runs into the apartment in a flurry of excitement, tosses his briefcase on the ground, and announces to his mother as he stands on the threshold: "Today, Tanya was so roaring at recess." These young ladies are on the verge of shedding a tear already. It is essential that the discussion be brought to a close at this time. Convince the youngster that the tears of other people, particularly the sorrow felt by his friends, should not be disregarded by him in any way. After that, the student will be overjoyed when a fellow student receives five, will be really distressed when another person is unhappy, and will be willing to offer a fellow student something that is very important to him.

What happens, though, if the son does not treat the girl in the manner that the parents would prefer?

Natasha was a frail and sickly young lady who lived in the same neighborhood as Petya. In addition to this, she exhibited a great deal of cowardice, which Petya did not appreciate at all.

Petya made the decision to instill courage in Natasha in his own way, and he was successful to the point where she was not frightened to pick up a live mouse. He accomplished this goal by secretly placing a frog inside one of her pockets. The young lady went pale and was so shaken by her experience that she did not emerge from the safety of her home for several days. The manner in which Petya's mother dealt with the situation exemplified intelligence and tact.

People in the Soviet Union had a natural tendency toward collectivism, which manifests itself as a sense of mutual aid and help, comradery, egalitarianism, responsiveness, and concern for others. When both boys and girls participate together in the laborious procedures of cleaning the yard, playgrounds, and so on, all of these attributes can be formed more easily and in a shorter amount of time.

Engage Her In Fantasy Roleplaying

Have some fun messing with her head, and don't stop enjoying yourselves in the process. Maintain your mystique while avoiding the appearance of being too strange to be human. If there is anything that she need from you, make it difficult for her to obtain it. Don't put too much weight on what happens. Keep in mind that the art of seduction is the oldest form of entertainment in the annals of human history.

One Who Is Able To Listen

One must always remember the importance of having strong listening skills. To truly understand what she is trying to convey, you must pay attention not only to the words she uses but also to the underlying message. There are many instances in which women say one thing when they truly intend something another. Every woman craves the companionship of a man who can read her mind and know exactly what she's thinking, sometimes even before she opens her mouth to speak.

You certainly can say that women have unreasonable demands and expectations of themselves.

The key is to understand that falling in love is not about you and never will be about you; rather, it is all about the person you are falling in love with.

Humor

Possessing a healthy sense of humor is undeniably a significant asset in any situation. One thing that can go to a woman's heart like nothing else can is a good laugh. As a result of the stressful environment in which we live, many women feel the need to release their tension through humor. It's beneficial to have an alpha male quality, but it's much more advantageous to have a strong sense of humor.

How to Be an Effective Listener

You absolutely need to possess this as one of the most significant qualities you can. Every woman craves the company of a man who will listen to her thoughts and feelings, even if they are illogical. There are a lot of males that try to listen, but they don't really pay attention.

The majority of women have several thoughts. Some are perfectly reasonable, while others are completely deranged.

An intimate connection is formed between two people when a lady feels she can open up to you about everything, including her wildest fantasies, without fear of judgment. She would realize deep down in her being that she longs for you and that she cannot live without you. In point of fact, she may even start to depend on you, to the point where she feels as if she needs to share every single thought she has with you. There is nothing more gratifying than having a woman open up to you about her life. Also, keep in mind that if you have earned her trust to the point that she is prepared to divulge all of her thoughts to you, this indicates that she is also eager to divulge everything else, including her body, to you as well.

Taking Turns At Happiness And Setting Limits

It's possible that you'll find this strange, but part of honoring limits is ensuring that everyone involved is happy. We are so filled with joy that we can hardly wait to spread the good vibes to everyone around us. If there is happiness to be had in this life, then we owe it to one another to spread that happiness around, don't you think? When it's too enormous, we get the feeling that we want to talk about it with everyone in the entire world.

When we talk about happy events that we've had, we anticipate a positive reaction from the people with whom we're communicating. We are looking forward to a response that is both uplifting and inspirational. We certainly wouldn't be content with an alternative kind of response at this point, would we?

When someone doesn't respond in the way that we anticipate they will, it might leave us feeling perplexed and even irrationally angry. Our close friends ought to be overjoyed for us, don't you think? Either they will fulfill their responsibility, or they will not be considered our pals.

Oh well, our self-centered egotism causes us to forget that we shouldn't only be concerned with ourselves but also with the welfare of others. It could be a good idea to check in with the other person first and see how they are doing. Perhaps we should hold off on sharing what we had planned to communicate until a later time? Can we make someone else envious of us?

A friend of mine recently returned from an extremely pricey vacation. When I inquired further about her thoughts, she said that she did not find anything noteworthy about the experience. In my thoughts, I heard myself saying, "Well, that's a good answer, and that's the mantra of wealthy and intelligent people." They are conscious that their actions can inspire envy in others, so they make it a point to refrain from doing so. Dealing with people who don't always have access to the same resources you do in a human and kind manner is essential while doing business with them.

When someone asks you about the price of the shoes that you have just purchased, it may be a good idea to take a moment to think and then respond with something along the lines of "I don't remember" or "They were a gift" or something like. It is impolite to brag about one's own children in front of a couple who is unable to have children of their own. It is absurd to brag in great detail about the mansion you own to a person who is having trouble making even the most fundamental of rent arrangements.

In most cases, the main difficulty is what we believe of ourselves, rather than what others think of us. We dislike having to be considerate of the dignity of another person. Even if it is one of the happiest things that has ever happened to us, we need to be careful about how much we share with other people and how much we share with strangers who become our allies.

This is a problem that many people in this day and age face. When something good happens to them, they get joyful, but when something unpleasant happens to them, they become shaken. When feelings become uncontrollable, a release valve is required so that they can be released. The ultimate consequence is living in a permanent state of emotional burps and expecting the people closest to you to be able to deal with and understand such conduct.

Have a conversation with your daughter about how different experiences each have their own unique value and significance. A person who is spiritually balanced is aware that everything in the universe is in a constant state of flux, and because of this, it is impossible to say whether something that has happened to us was a positive or negative experience.

We are not aware of what is beyond the horizon. Our perception extends to the periphery of our consciousness and incorporates the event that has most recently taken place for us. We shouldn't dump the contents of the bucket of our stories on the heads of those who are closest to us or the most removed from us.

One of the most important talents that your daughter can learn to develop is the ability to listen. Anyone can engage in self-referential discourse. To grow as individuals, we must frequently learn to incorporate the joy of others into our own sense of fulfillment.

It is not always the wisest course of action to throw a party for a person who is grieving the loss of a loved one. Sometimes the thing that brings us the most happiness is the thing that causes the most suffering for someone else. It does not necessarily imply that the other person is malicious or envious; rather, it may imply that we have been insensitive or disrespectful.

Find a small group of people who are pleased to receive your joy and share it with them. When doing so, exercise discretion and care.

Indicator Sexual Gps 1 – Connect To Your Satellite:

Know the terrain well before you get into bed with someone, or even before you begin that initial flirtation, so you can make the most of the experience.

What exactly does this entail?

Simply put, it implies being aware of what you are agreeing to and identifying the conditions that cannot be met. What do you hope to gain from this relationship? Is this a casual hookup or the beginning of a more committed relationship that will eventually lead to marriage? Do both of them have the same idea of where they are and do they agree on it?

An important first step in orienting your sexual GPS toward excellent sex is to take an inventory of your own wishes. It is impossible to have good sex when each individual wants something different from their partner. Taking an inventory of your personal needs is an important first step.

Now, lest you get the wrong idea, I'm not at all going to join on the bandwagon of monogamy being the default option. I've spent some time in Monogamy Town and had some enjoyable sexual experiences there. And I've gotten some good sex while partying at the Meat Market, where I've also sport-fucked with the best of them.

It is not for me to decide which option is superior; that decision lies solely with you. Being at ease with what you want and being honest about it with both yourself and any potential partner(s) you're contemplating is a crucial step in the process. Everyone needs to be on the same page regarding the circumstances before they can enjoy satisfying sexual encounters.

Indicator No. 2 of the Sexual GPS: Choose Your Path

As soon as you have established what kind of experience you are searching for, it will be a lot simpler for you to find someone else who is looking for the exact same thing as you. And because you won't have to deal with any of the pointless drama that comes with pursuing someone who doesn't want the same thing you want, you'll be able to make better and more productive decisions about how and where to spend your time.

Sexual GPS sign 3: investigate your surroundings.

Yes, I am referring to the body of your companion (at long last!).

At this point, based on your past make out sessions and flirtations, you should have a pretty good sense of how they like to be touched, where on their body they are ticklish, and whether or not they enjoy being tickled, teased, or stroked ever so little...

Now is the moment to step up your game to the next level.

Focus your powers of observation on your partner's breath, on how their pupils expand with pleasure when you stroke or kiss that particular place, on the blush of their skin as their arousal peaks, and on the shifting rhythm of their strokes as they approach climax. Dedicate your powers of observation to the study of your partner's breath.

Study every facet of their sexual response, and of course, adapt in accordance with their guidance. However, if you are as meticulous a student of your partner's reactions and responses as you are at memorizing all of those Game of Thrones subplots, you will be the one who is recognized as an amazing lover.

Sexually-Oriented Global Positioning System indication 4: Detours and alternative paths

It is time to switch things up a bit now that you are an expert at reading your partner's sexual cues; try a different position or take the opposite role; if you are typically the dominant one, try being the submissive; if you always wait for your partner to initiate, surprise them for once and jump their bones; if you always wait for your partner to initiate, surprise them for once and jump their bones. If you aren't typically the romantic type, pull out all the stops and plan a night that is as mushy and sentimental as any Sandra Bullock film (you knew we weren't done talking about her).

Don't forget to have fun and maintain a flowing spirit of exploration at all times.

Your creativity and the amount of lubricant you have on hand are the only things that can stop you from having a nice time in the bedroom.

What Should I Put on?

Some individuals have the misconception that you need to dress in really revealing and provocative clothing. Instead, you should put on something that is not too tight and is comfortable, and you should also make an effort to wear something that makes you feel good. Some individuals choose to dress in a manner that is symbolic of particular deities or the east. However, it has the potential to bring the practice of tantra into the bedroom.

However, before beginning to practice tantra, you should first make it a priority to clean up your act and be content with who you are.

Before you move on to the next step, you should begin by brushing your teeth and your hair. This is a speedy and straightforward way to truly boost your confidence and make it easier for you to carry out the task at hand.

You are not required to take a pre-ritual bath, despite the fact that this is something that many people choose to do before they begin. You need to make sure that it is somewhat structured, and that your goal is to ensure that you are bonded, but not bonded sufficiently to have sex just yet. You should wash each other in ways that are not sexual, and you should use scented soaps and oils. This creates excitement and anticipation between the two of you, and it's also something that you'll like doing along with the other person.

You should engage in activities together that not only build excitement but also heighten your sense of anticipation for one another. In the end, this will be beneficial to both of you, and it will bring about an experience that is both noble and artistic with your spouse.

Putting You in the Picture

You should prepare the atmosphere by incorporating rituals into sexual activity, and you should also make sure that your location is prepared. The majority of individuals concentrate on ensuring that there is a significant amount of white in the space, which might come in the form of cushions, candles, and also quiet music. You should carry out these actions with the goal of elevating the sex experience to a higher level.

The majority of individuals simply dash into the bedroom without putting much effort into establishing the appropriate ambiance. However, you should try your hand at decorating it if you truly want to make it stand out in both of your memories of the event. A better and more intimate experience between the two of you can be achieved with the assistance of music that is gentle and seductive. Music is fantastic for sex in general, but listening to gentle, sensuous music can affect the way that sex is experienced for both partners and will also bring about a sense of understanding, wellness, and happiness.

Take a Deep Breath!

Before you do anything else, you need to be sure that you are breathing correctly and that the manner you do it is beneficial to you. This is an effective method for calming your mind and helping you relax your body, so give it a try. What you need to do is take a deep breath in through your nose, make sure your belly is completely full of air, and then let out your breath. You should be able to feel your belly expanding outwardly. You are breathing using your diaphragm, and you really ought to make it a point to concentrate on breathing in this manner as much as possible. Exhaling should cause the belly to begin returning to its normal size, so keep an eye on it.

If you are having trouble with this, you should imagine pressing the pelvis down through there, and then pushing the breath directly to the floor. This will help you improve your posture. Make an effort to do this a few times before you try to do it during sex so that it may become more natural to you and you can experience the full benefits of this as well.

Consider getting a massage.

Last but not least, you should attempt rubbing yourself before engaging in sexual activity. These massages don't have to go very long, but you should make an effort to take turns being the one who gives and receives the leisurely massage. You may ask your spouse to rub your feet for a couple of minutes, and then let them do anything they want for a couple of minutes while they stroke your feet.

During each player's turn, you should not be afraid to provide the necessary input to the other players. It is acceptable to point out to your partner what it is that they could improve upon, and doing so will assist them in truly giving you what it is that you desire.

This is a challenge that almost all couples eventually face. You will have a far better chance of getting what you want if you communicate with the other person. Communication is something that the vast majority of individuals need to realize is essential to having. The manner in which you cooperate is an excellent educational opportunity for you. You will be able to teach your partner what you want, and they will teach you what they want, which will result in the most satisfying sexual encounter for you that is humanly possible.

You should focus on how their hands feel on you, the manner they touch you, and the sensuous quality of this experience, and then use that as a springboard to relax both your body and your mind. Your capacity to deal with it will improve as a result of this, and you will become happier and more successful than you have been in the past as a result.

In addition to the fact that it is found in the fluids of the body, testosterone is responsible for a wide variety of additional roles and effects in the body. Even though the chemical mechanisms that lead to hair loss in men and women are not completely understood, it has been blamed for excessive hair loss (also known as androgenetic alopecia, the medical term).

The ovaries of females and the testes of males both generate this hormone, but the testes of males produce a far greater quantity of it. Not only are different kinds of mental conduct susceptible to influence by the environment and by one's genetics, but also by the day-to-day fluctuations in hormone levels. For instance, stress can prevent the body from producing testosterone, which can then result in lower quantities of the hormone being secreted.

There has been some positive development in recent times. Recent research has found that one of the best ways to keep stress at bay is to regularly engage in sexual activity that involves penile penetration and vaginal penetration. Unfortunately, a large number of people in all areas of life report that when they are stressed, they lose the desire to have sex and even experience negative side effects like sexual dysfunction as a result of this.

According to the findings of an insightful study (Biological Psychology, volume 71, page 214), having sex, and more specifically intimate sexual contact, is a significantly more efficient method of relieving stress than other sexual activities, such as masturbation. Because sexual activity is associated with lower blood pressure and lower levels of stress, it leads to improvements in both psychological and physiological performance.

In addition, orgasms experienced by women during penile-vaginal intercourse are beneficial for physiological behavior, whereas orgasms experienced during other forms of sexual activity are not as beneficial. It is recommended that those of us who suffer from public speaking anxiety, often known as stage fright, engage in sexual activity (although not on stage, of course), as this has been shown to reduce feelings of tension and anxiety.

Some researchers believe that when a couple makes love, the neurotransmitter oxytocin that is released helps to calm the body, which in turn lowers blood pressure and prevents stress. Oxytocin is a hormone that is produced in the brain as well as in other organs such as the ovaries and the testes. Oxytocin levels are thought to drop dramatically during stressful situations, and the fact that administering the hormone to animal models alleviates stress, pointing to the possibility that it plays a part in the regulation of some physiological responses to stress.

Because of research of such high quality and the absence of public stress reduction programs, such as screenings conducted by government agencies with the goals of enhancing recognition and treatment as well as lowering levels of stress and depression, primary prevention has become essential.

Penetrative penal-vaginal sex could be a major method for the avoidance of stress, given that stress and depression have become more prevalent disorders that are associated with a wide range of significant and unwelcome side effects in both men and women.

The idea that women should only be able to experience orgasm through vaginal activity is one of the most widespread misconceptions concerning the female orgasm.

This is not at all the case, but it is a common misconception that, for a very long time, has led us to disregard the sexual requirements that women have. The origin of this misconception may be traced back to Sigmund Freud, the founder of psychoanalysis. Freud was the first person to realize that clitoral stimulation was an easy way for women to achieve orgasm.

Freud thought that this kind of stimulation was immature and believed that it was critical for women to grow more sexually mature by concentrating solely on vaginal stimulation in order to obtain orgasms. He regarded this form of stimulation as being "juvenile."

The issue is that the vagina was not intended to be used for sexual acts like orgasms. It does not have the densely packed nerve endings that are seen, for example, in the clitoris or in the head of the penis.

As a consequence of Freud's conclusion, it was assumed that women who were unable to have orgasm as a result of having sexual relations with another woman had some kind of mental defect. In an effort to "liberate" women from their need on the clitoris for sexual pleasure, a wide variety of techniques have been developed throughout the years.

Only in the recent decades has society started openly discussing women's rights to have sex whenever and however they like, including the ability to experience orgasm in any way that works for them.

One further prevalent fallacy concerning the female orgasm is the idea that only women can fake orgasms.

Even though this book is on female orgasms, I believe it is vital for both men and women to understand that orgasms do not occur during every sexual experience. This is something that both men and women need to be aware of. Approximately one-fifth of males have admitted to having staged an orgasm with a partner at some point in their lives. They are motivated to lie for the same reason that women do, which is that they do not want their spouses to feel let down.

Orgasms aren't always easy to come by when you're in a relationship. Since we are familiar with our bodies and the sensations that result from masturbation, we have no doubt that we will be able to stop ourselves each and every time. Our sexual partners are required to acquire this knowledge over the course of time and, more crucially, with our assistance.

Once more, pretending to have an orgasm is not the answer for either sexual orientation. It does nothing but make the situation more complicated and inhibits both people from having a sexual session that is truly rewarding.

Have you been paying less attention to your sexual life as of late? It's not like you don't care at all, but finding the time and energy to do so can be challenging. It may appear to be difficult on some days due to the fact that there is work, cleaning, working out, grocery shopping, meal preparation, laundry, children, obligations to family and friends, and ironing.

I force myself to shake the all-too-familiar attraction that my body is secretly carrying for me despite my best efforts. It appears that my defensive barriers are the superior choice.

The fact that you haven't had a new hairstyle in seven years isn't exactly an indication that you've grown up, but whatever.

Even after all this time, those darn bangs continue to make my sex tingle, continue to make it difficult for me to breathe, and continue to make me want to be the woman to whom he directs his smoldering gaze as he glances through them.

But sadly, I am his stepsister, and he only recently acquired me in a charity auction, so we might as well get started on making amends right away. At least mum won't be upset about it.

I move out of the way to give him some space in the restricted area. If he chooses to do so, he can remain there.

My next step ought to take me around him, but instead he clutches my wrist in a kind manner. I am being jolted by an electric current. Oh God, you should see what happens when he touches my body. It's completely absurd. He tightens his hold, and I feel myself being pulled back.

"What?" I inquire while averting my eyes from you.

"Hey." How is it that a single phrase with such a gentle and low tone can get past all of my defenses?

My eyes are drawn upward. The gaze of James meets mine. Although it's not quite a burning look, it certainly is intense. Then, after looking up at the ceiling for a moment, he tilts his head ever-so-slightly and returns his gaze to me. He gives a wicked grin that spreads across his lips.

It is not necessary for me to look up in order to determine what he was looking at. My mind is pondering the following question: Why is James, of all people, bringing attention to the fact that we are in the vicinity of some mistletoe?

"Not interested." I decline to accept his offer.

"But I know how much you adore mistletoe."

"I do. However, you made it quite plain on the Christmas after my eighteenth birthday that you would rather kiss a cactus than kiss me under the mistletoe. This was a particularly terrible realization for me.

"Yeah... well, I guess I messed up. And even if what I said was accurate, I should be ashamed of myself for saying it. Permit me to demonstrate that I have grown up. The tone of his voice has undisclosed substances that are guaranteed to melt your underwear.

Since I can feel Heath and Ford's gaze penetrating me, I can only assume that they are witnessing whatever it is that

Ford and Heath are currently engaged in.

The rest of the world begins to slip away, and all that is left in my mind is how badly I want to kiss James. Am I quickly forgetting how badly I wanted a kiss from him at that disastrous Christmas party, but he refused to give it to me in front of all of his friends and family? Has the insanity of my imagination not taught me anything?

I give in to his efforts and permit him to pull me closer till the lengths of our bodies are touching. I give in to his efforts and enable him to bring me closer. My body has the uncontrollable want to crane my neck to look into his dark brown eyes.

There is absolutely no sense of brotherhood there. This has got to be some kind of joke. If I'm going to have to resort to Plan E, which stands for Escape, I had well get moving quickly.

Acknowledging One's Physical Maturity While Taking Ownership Of One's Body

In some respects, reaching the age of physical maturity is a simple task. It takes place regardless of whether we want it to or not, and we have very little influence over the rate at which it occurs. The pituitary gland, which sits at the base of the brain, acts as a timekeeper, helping to determine what will grow and when it will develop.

But the process of aging physically is also challenging because it is typically so awkward: new hair grows, voices change, bodies transform, skin becomes oily, and underarms become odorous. Hormones are dispersed in every direction.

They get to choose what part of their physical body only belongs to them, what they are not "giving away" (unless abuse is a factor, which we will discuss in a later chapter); however, it is important for them to realize that there is one specific aspect of physical maturity over which they have sole control. While a teen may feel frustrated and helpless when it comes to the development of his or her body, it is important for them to realize that there is one specific aspect of physical maturity over which they have sole control. This is not just an opportunity for them, but also a responsibility.

Knowing that they have power over anything can be an exciting notion for many developing adolescents, but this feeling is amplified when the topic at hand is something as crucial as their sexual health. As their parents, we can facilitate their growth in this area of empowerment by assisting them in the establishment of appropriate boundaries and encouraging them to commit to adhering to those boundaries.

It's likely that you're familiar with the proverb that goes, "If you aim at nothing, you will hit it every time." It is extremely unlikely that a kid will be able to maintain healthy sexual boundaries if they do not first establish some appropriate sexual limits for themselves. A fairly mature decision for a teenager to make is to establish a physical boundary. A physical border provides a tangible purpose with relationship implications, and this in turn instantly brings the psychological and social components of existence into play.

Create your plans for the future through texting.

After all of that, one is going to run out of things to talk about, which is especially likely if one is told not to leave the house unless it is absolutely necessary to do so for some reason. A fantastic way to engage the person you're interested in romantically and make him or her excited about the future is to make plans together about potential date ideas for the future.

Discuss your go-to eatery or a pastime in the great outdoors that you adore, and you never know when you could find someone else who shares your enthusiasm! Even better, send them a virtual invitation to a date via the internet. An unusual date concept could be having a virtual date while watching a movie or cooking together. Another possibility is going on a hike together.

Clarify it for me.

Because vocal and non-verbal cues of communication are absent from text-based exchanges, users of this mode of communication may find themselves misunderstood more quickly. When someone reads a text message, they may interpret the words as if they were saying something else entirely. Pay close attention to the message that you are trying to convey in order to avoid creating any unnecessary confusion.

Subtle details, like as the amount of time it takes you to react to something, may send a message to the reader about the perceived level of interest. Even if you are unable to respond because you are preoccupied with work or stuck in a meeting, it is important that you communicate this to your partner so that they do not waste their time trying to determine whether or not you are still interested in the relationship.

It's possible that getting a text message will make you feel excited or that it will be an annoying nuisance. If you follow these rules, there is a good chance that you will be able to go on a fruitful path that will allow you to build and deepen a nascent relationship when we are going through a time of social separation. Instead of waiting for a more ideal time to connect, you should make the most of any opportunity that presents itself.

You Are The Most Important Thing In Her Life.

It does not take much guts to love someone, but it does take a lot of bravery to commit to spending your entire life with that person.

Don't let her get used to you just so you may ditch her later. Do not let her become accustomed to taking to you each day and then, all of a sudden, stop doing so.

Don't let her become accustomed to seeing you whenever she wants, because then you'll have to surprise her by telling her that you don't have time for her.

Don't get her used to flirting with you so that you may turn around and treat her like she has no value to you at some point in the future.

Do not let her become accustomed to the fact that you would always be there for her and then, on the day when she requires your assistance, fail to be anywhere to be found.

Do not condition her to anticipate that you would treat her as though she is someone exceptional and then, all of a sudden, behave in an unmannerly manner toward her. This will only set her up for disappointment.

Please don't get her used to depending on you and then, when she needs you the most, disappoint her by letting her down when she's already relied on you the most.

Do not let her become accustomed to hearing you say that you miss her and then, all of a sudden, stop making an effort to show her that you care about her. Please don't get her used to hearing you say that you love her and then, all of a sudden, give her the impression that you never gave a damn about her in the first place after doing so.

DO NOT DEPART FROM HER IN SUCH A STATE. YOU ARE THE MOST IMPORTANT THING IN HER LIFE.

The past does not dictate our future.

Even if we have a history that we don't feel especially good about, that doesn't imply that we can't go on to create a brighter future for ourselves.

At first, you won't believe your eyes. A surge of feelings coupled with a sensation of calm and contentment, all of which occur simultaneously. They will provide you with an experience that no one else has been able to provide up to this point. Your entire sensory experience will be heightened. You won't feel incomplete for the very first time in a very extended period of time. You will have the sensation that life once again makes sense to you.

Before you begin weaving and knotting, additional dreams will come to you, and each one will shatter your heart more completely than the last.

It will leave you feeling burned, bewildered, and, worst of all, it will make you feel trapped and angry with yourself for allowing this to happen again. You will feel trapped and upset with yourself for allowing this to happen again.

You will never, ever be required to feel that way.

I beg you, do not forget about all of the nights that you sobbed until there were no more tears left in your eyes. Remember the reasons why you decided to end the relationship. Do not let yourself forget how they submerged you in all of their problems and how they suffocated you in their poisonous energy.

Do not, under any circumstances, let yourself forget about that agony, that agonizing suffering that was brought on by them and that left you feeling so shattered that you were powerless and empty.

Remember that someone who cares about you and loves you will never, ever do anything to hurt you, and you should never forget this.

In addition to this, supposing that they genuinely love you or that they do care is an even more distressing scenario.

This indicates that they will never love anyone else more than themselves. That indicates that they have not yet resolved their problems, and as long as they have not done so, they will continue to use you as their emotional punching bag.

Because you are wonderful and powerful, they will always utilize you to make themselves feel better. In addition, they are aware of the depth of your affection for them. They are aware, even to themselves, that you will always take them back.

As soon as they went, you had a feeling deep down in your gut that it was actually the best thing that could have happened. In your subconscious, you were aware that the fact that this person was no longer in your life was fortunate for you because it allowed you to make room in your heart and life for someone new, someone better, a love that is more special, and someone who deserves you. Someone who cheers you up at all times, not just when they are in a good mood or when it is convenient for them to do so is a person who is consistently positive.

You are worthy of a partner who does not cause you to experience internal tensions. When things get difficult, when life gets confusing, when you are lost and bewildered and unsure of what to do next, there is someone who is there for you who will never leave your side. Someone who will never abandon you when you are caught in the rain, whether it be literal rain or the rain of tears. Someone who is unmoved no matter how many people are attempting to catch their attention, since deep down they understand that what they have with you is something that only comes around once in a person's lifetime.

I am aware of the fact that you adore them, and I am also aware of the fact that they may have encouraged you at a time when you were unsure of yourself. I am aware that they were your closest companion. I am aware that you have shared every detail of your history with them, even the names of everyone who has caused you pain. They wiped away your tears and kissed those aspects of yourself that you have never showed to anyone else. About all the things you did that you are ashamed of, all the things you do not like about yourself, and all the things that make you, you. About everything that makes you, you. About everything that makes you, you.

They cherished your heart, which is why it is so challenging to let them go and not carry it back with you. You shared something unique, and the connection that you had will continue to exist. I am aware.

Nevertheless, I am aware that they wanted things to be done in their own particular manner, and that the moment you began to challenge them is when the issues began to arise. I am aware that by the time everything was said and done, they left you in a broken state. I am aware that there was a purpose behind your breakup. I am aware of the suffering they inflicted upon you, as well as the lies that were told and the instances in which you felt disgusted with yourself for putting up with their toxic behavior.

In light of the fact that they will inevitably return, kindly keep all of this in mind. Because I guarantee that if someone is selfish, if someone has taken away your joy and damaged your life in the past, they will continue to do so in the future.

Keep an open heart and mind for the love that you so richly deserve; I can assure you that it is out there waiting for you. TO YOU, & FOREVER MORE. Simply be who and what you are.

Conversation Strategies: 10 Strategies To Help Communicate Between With Your Teen To Talk About Sex.

1. Starting a conversation with your adolescent as early as possible and making sure to keep it going.

When you start talking to your child at a young age and ensure that the dialogue is not limited to a single occasion, you are laying the groundwork for a lifetime of healthy communication.

It teaches kids more about having self-respect, being sensitive and having an acceptable touch when it comes to other members of the family, and what kind of limits they ought to have.

Your child will begin to perceive this topic as an important component of the core values you want to impart in her if you make it a point to talk about it on a regular basis. This will make it much simpler to have a conversation about sexuality with your child once they reach puberty and begin to experience sexual feelings themselves.

When it comes to adolescents, it is much simpler for them to talk about the values and safety, which makes it possible to have this discussion as an ongoing conversation rather than merely talking as a reaction to an event that took place at that particular time.

Because of this, it is quite easy to feel at ease when engaging in conversations on a regular basis.

Instead, what takes place is if these conversations do not need to take place on a specific occasion, such as a first date or prom night. The purpose of these conversations is merely to educate you and encourage you to give careful consideration to the choices you will make.

If it is coming from the place of an emergency talk that has been held, then it will be seen as a manner of seeking to control them or demanding that they do or avoid specific things.

This would only result in disaster for you in the long run.

If you believe that you may have been too late to have these kinds of talks with your teenage child, you need to make sure that you talk about the reasons why you are having such conversations and avoid telling them that it is more like a demand or rule that you are building up for them. If you feel that you may have been too late to have these kinds of conversations with your teenage child, you need to make sure that you have these conversations. It is all about providing assistance to them in order to keep them safe, both physically and psychologically.

2. Place a Greater Emphasis on Your Values.

Teens have access to a wide variety of resources that can educate them on a variety of topics, including those pertaining to puberty and development, the workings of sexuality, and challenges associated with these stages of life.

It might have come up in their health lesson; other possible sources include books and the internet.

The most important thing for you to focus on, though, is making sure that kids acquire the ideals associated with healthy sexuality from you.

If you do not take this step, you are merely giving your child the opportunity to learn these things from the internet, television, and music.

And if proper precautions are not taken, they could learn about sexuality and sex from pornographic websites on the internet, which could provide them with an upsetting depiction of sex and sexuality that you might want to show them.

They can also learn from their peers, and even while part of what they learn might be beneficial, it won't be backed up with life experience. This is why you need to be there for them to instill such ideals to them surrounding sex and sexuality. They can learn from their peers.

You're In TheFriendzone If... These Texts Keep Coming Up

The practice of friendzoning is disgusting. Guys will try whatever they can to avoid being friendzoned because they are aware of how damaging it can be to their egos if they are, but there are instances when there is nothing they can do to stop it from happening. The fact that the friendzone is almost always a covert murderer makes dealing with it all the more difficult. But there's no need to be concerned since we've got your back!

The focus of this chapter will be on the factors that lead to guys being friendzoned via text.

It takes an Eternity for Her to Reply.

If you've been attempting to grab a girl's attention and she's been taking an extremely long time to answer, it's probably because she doesn't like you very much. Women are not as subtle about their intentions as men are, so if she is leading you on by giving you an inch when all you want is a mile, then it's time to reevaluate what it is that you want to accomplish in this relationship. It's possible that a woman won't react right away because she's concerned that her guy will see her silence as an indication that she wants more than just a platonic relationship with him if he responds too quickly. Alternatively, she might be considering how best to deny your request without offending you in any way. If she takes an extremely long time to react, it's probably because she's not interested in the first place; in this case, you'd be better off finding someone else who is interested.

You are either her brother or her closest friend, she says.

There are a lot of women who will try to "play hard to get," but if the girl you want calls you her brother or her closest friend, then it's probable that she isn't interested in anything more than developing a friendship with you. If she feels that she can't be honest with you, then it is probably because she doesn't want to hurt your feelings. However, the fact is that if a lady you like calls you her brother, then it is time for you to let her go. If she feels that she can't be honest with you, then it is probably because she doesn't want to hurt your feelings. There are lots of other women who would like to date you, so don't take it personally if she doesn't want to.

Avoiding and Avoiding the Compliments Received

The majority of men are aware that women enjoy receiving compliments; hence, if a woman consistently avoids offering you compliments and opts, instead, to give you a casual pat on the back, this is a clear indication that she is not interested in you. This can be taken as a hint that she is not interested in pursuing anything more than friendship, but if you keep trying to acquire something more, then eventually she will have to say something and let you down gently. If you keep trying to get something else, then soon she will have to say something and let you down gently.

She does her best to avoid phone calls.

If the girl you like acts as though she is trying to avoid phone calls, it is likely because she does not want to spend any additional time with you. If a woman is interested in a man, she will seize every opportunity to spend time with him, even if it's only for a short period of time, such as an hour. If she is not picking up the phone when you contact her, then it is quite likely that she is not interested in you in any way other than as a friend, and it is time for you to move on.

It is important for you, as a parent, to have a firm grasp on the sexual values and beliefs that you wish to instill in your children before you are compelled to do so. Ideally, you should do this well in advance.

For instance, you and your partner ought to be clear on your attitudes on contraception before either of you brings your adolescent daughter to get her contraceptive implant implanted. This is something that you should accomplish before either of you takes her.

Or, before you begin a conversation with your three-year-old child about the appropriate level of clothing to wear in the home, consider how you and your partner feel about the presence of nudity.

It is completely worthless for us to instruct our children about sexuality if we do not communicate to them our own sexual goals and notions.

What are some of the sexual norms and attitudes that you hold?

A profound awareness of something that is significant to us might serve as a personal compass to direct how we go about living our lives. Our thoughts, feelings, actions, and words all shed light on them. When it comes to particular principles, we frequently have very strong feelings. At other times, we might not even be aware that we hold particular principles to be true.

It could be considered a value that sexual activity should never take place outside the context of a committed romantic relationship like marriage.

Attitudes can be defined as a person's thoughts and sentiments regarding what is considered to be excellent, horrible, right, or incorrect.

One point of view holds that sexual engagement should not begin for adolescents until they have reached the age of majority in their respective countries.

The definition of values offered by the author Al Vernacchio is "the deepest set of laws that influence one's decisions."

It is not natural for us to have certain values and attitudes. Since our principles are individual to us, we decide for ourselves which ones we wish to believe in. They change as we do as we become older. The lessons we learn about them come from our ancestors, our culture, and our surroundings. It is typical for our values to alter throughout time as a result of the various experiences we encounter that put them to the test.

The Technique Of Starting A Conversation Without Fear Of Being Rejected

It's possible that having the ability to approach people could be the deciding factor between leading an active life in which you get what you want and leading a quiet life in which you don't get what you want. The majority of individuals are content to let chance choose who comes into their lives. Why not grab hold of life by the horns and determine your own course of events? Why should we trust chance to determine the path? People have no idea how to approach other people, which is why approaching people is the most difficult activity involving social skills. I am confident that everyone would agree with me that this is the case. It is possible to avoid rejection by utilizing the appropriate strategy in the appropriate setting.

There are many different angles from which one can approach an individual or a group of individuals. There is no such thing as a universal method that can be applied to all situations. I strongly disagree with the usage of pickup lines or anything else of a similar nature because most individuals are able to see right through them. The population is already quite watchful. If you want to get a date with someone, the last thing you want to do is turn them off by using corny pickup lines. The method has one and only one goal, and that is to get the person you are having the conversation with to pause for a moment and pay attention to what it is that you are saying. This pretty much wraps up everything. Transitioning to a new topic and maintaining engagement in the conversation are two whole separate stages that will be discussed in later chapters.

For the time being, I want you to consider a successful strategy any one in which the subject of your conversation (for lack of a better word) pauses and acknowledges what it is that you are saying. Even if the individual continues to walk away after you say anything to them and they stop and ask "What?", you can still consider this a successful interaction. This is due to the fact that the beginning of each engagement may be broken down into three parts, which are as follows:

The approach that was taken.

The next step, which is to have a conversation about it

Keeping the natural progression of the conversation.

You will learn how to master each of these stages by reading this book, and as a result, you will be able to attain your goals more swiftly and effortlessly.

People have a hard time differentiating between each of these stages, and as a result, they incorrectly believe that they are all part of the same stage. Because of this, they are led to believe that the method is the most frightening of the three options. People, in my opinion, hurt themselves more than they help themselves because all they can see is complete and utter failure. Instead, one can be objective and pinpoint what aspect of the approach can be improved. For example, if I get rejected after a person stops and acknowledges what I am saying but keeps on walking, because I said something totally irrelevant, I acknowledge that the approach was perfect but the transition, on the other hand, was where I failed. By segmenting each stage, it is a lot easier to dissect the good from the bad and ultimately improve much more quickly through objective self-assessment.

To ensure the highest success rate for your approach, I will give you four ways of approaching people that will not only help calm your nerves, but will also get the person to stop and acknowledge what you are saying.

Having A Conversation About Gender Identity

Parenting and figuring out one's gender identity can both be challenging issues to work through. As a parent, you naturally want to make decisions that are in your child's best interest.

There are a few aspects that should be kept in mind in relation to gender identification.

It is essential to keep in mind that gender and sex are not synonymous terms in any way, shape, or form. The term "gender" relates to the social and cultural expectations surrounding how a person should behave, whereas the term "sexuality" refers to the biological traits of an individual.

It is not necessary for a person to identify with a particular gender simply because they are born with certain traits associated with either gender.

It is also essential to have a firm grasp on the fact that one's gender identification cannot be changed. It is something that people experience on the deepest level within themselves and cannot change.

The first and most crucial step in being an excellent parent is coming to terms with your child's gender identification.

Being willing to compromise and show understanding is the most important thing.

The road of parenting while struggling with gender identity can be a challenging one, but it is essential to keep in mind that you are not alone.

Your role as a parent gives you a great deal of sway in determining the gender identity that your child will develop.

Your role as a parent is to assist your youngster in comprehending and expressing their gender in a manner that is satisfactory for them.

Your child's education should include up-to-date information about gender roles and identities, as this is one of the most essential things you can do for them.

Because of this, it will be easier for individuals to make educated decisions concerning their own identity. In addition to this, it is essential to provide your kid with unconditional love and acceptance no matter what decisions they make concerning their gender identification.

You can also play a part in forming your child's gender identification by setting a good example for them to follow in your own behavior. For instance, if you are a male who is at ease expressing his feminine side, this can inspire your son to do the same. If you are a woman, this can have the opposite effect.

If you are a woman who is self-assured in her femininity, you may find that this encourages your daughter to embrace the male aspects of her own identity.

The end goal of parenting is to produce a child who is not just physically and mentally sound but also content within their own skin. You may assist your child in achieving this objective by showing them love and support along the way.

Dealing with your child's confusion regarding their gender identity can be a challenging undertaking, but it is one that must be done correctly.

You are able to assist your child with comprehending and expressing their gender in a manner that is satisfactory for them if you use the appropriate strategy.

The following are some of the ways in which you can mold your child's gender identity:

1. Providing correct information regarding the various genders.

2. Offering encouragement and showing that you respect the decisions that your child has made

3. Setting a good example for others by your own positive actions

4. Providing your child with a setting that is both secure and encouraging. 5. Encouraging your child to be authentically themselves.

6. Instill in your youngster a sense of respect for other people.

7. assisting your youngster in becoming aware of their physical self as well as their emotions

8. Having age-appropriate conversations about puberty and its symptoms

9. Providing your child with the freedom to express their gender in a manner that is unique to them

10. Providing emotional and physical support to your child through challenging times

The Things That Men Want From Women

Just how difficult is it to win his approval?

The first thing you need to realize is that of all the creatures, men are the ones that can be satiated with the least amount of effort. Women are undoubtedly difficult, and unless you prove to her that you would do anything for her, she will continue to question the sincerity of your assertions on the depth of your affection for her.

Men have been accustomed to reading the signs, interpreting the intentions, and most importantly, according to the rules that are present with women, despite the fact that these norms are not explicitly stated. The majority of them do it cheerfully, anything he can do to communicate his feelings, to treat you like the jewel you are, and to compete with others for the opportunity to be the one for you.

It is possible that he will do all of that and even go to the moon and back for you, yet he will still fail to hit the mark. Why? Because having meaningful connections with others is never a one-way track. You have an urgent responsibility to locate a means by which you can make it halfway through this unknown voyage. Because of this, the relationship becomes more about the two of you and less about you individually.

Women frequently have a propensity to attribute men's conduct to their inherent nature, which arises from the fact that males are masculine. It's not uncommon to hear phrases like "that's how men are" or "he's a man, what do you expect?" in everyday conversation.

Now, this idea is a super killer and tremendously misconceived since often with men, it becomes the woman's attitude and approach that dictates his reaction, and not pre-determined factors. This is because men are more influenced by the woman's attitude and approach than they are by pre-determined forces.

What is it About You That Draws Him In?

Therefore, women have this mentality about men and sex, which is that the reason he is drawn to them is because they want their body. It is common knowledge that men are sexual beings; in their minds, physical appearance will always take precedence over any other factor. Therefore, a man needs to have a beautiful body, some appetizing aroma, a decent wit, and he should be good to go. There is no question that these characteristics will undoubtedly pique his interest; the question is, what will keep him around in the long run? Surprisingly, the majority of men will still opt for an annoying and half-witted woman merely because she is gorgeous; nevertheless, this only results in a fleeting adventure in which the woman continues to come out on top.

When a man is ready to start a serious relationship, whether it be marriage or just dating seriously, he is searching for qualities in a woman that are more substantial, more profound, and longer lasting. Sadly, the majority of women have a habit of hiding these characteristics earlier in a relationship, not realizing that these are the things that indefinitely drive a man on.

A self-assured, self-sufficient, independent, feminine, powerful, fun, and passionate woman who effortlessly appreciates her man's efforts and, most importantly, who values his friends just as much, that's what it takes to get the job done. You are looking to arouse him in every way possible, both emotionally and psychologically in addition to the more obvious way of turning him on physically.

What Contributes To A Decline In Attractiveness?

It can be a very draining experience on one's emotions to observe the flame of passion beginning to dim. But the first step in reigniting the fire that once burned between you and your partner is to figure out why you stopped finding your lover attractive in the first place. After identifying the root of the problem, you may next move on to devising a solution for it.

Talking to a trained emotional coach who is able to assist you in determining what factors led to you beginning to perceive your partner in a different light is the most effective method for determining why you have lost attraction in your relationship. The following are some of the most common factors that lead to a failed appeal attempt:

- Trying to conceal your anger or resentment – Trying to conceal your anger or resentment can cause you to lose interest in the relationship you're in. When expressing negative emotions, one should always do it in a composed and unequivocal manner.

- Is the quality of the conversation between you and your partner getting worse? Have you found that you and your partner talk about less and less meaningful or personal topics and more and more about practical matters? A failure in the ability to communicate effectively may result in a loss of attractiveness.

- Failing to share activities As your relationship progresses, you may find that you tend to settle into a routine and stop telling your partner about new experiences. This can be a problem because it can cause resentment. As a result of the absence of new experiences, you and your significant other can find that your interest in one another begins to wane.

- Letting go - It is wonderful to be at ease in a relationship; but, getting too at ease to the point where you start to let go, both physically and psychologically, is a surefire way to lose any intimacy you had with your partner. This can happen for a number of reasons.

- A loss of physical attraction can occur when you just stop finding your spouse physically appealing, which can result in a significant decrease in the amount of chemistry that exists between the two of you. However, solutions can be found for even these problems.

- Boredom - A decrease in attraction is another potential outcome of boredom. People have a natural yearning for new experiences, so when there are none to be had and a sense of familiarity begins to prevail, it can be simple for them to start losing interest in the relationship they are in.

- Merged identities - When you meet someone for the first time, you fall in love with them because of the unique qualities that they possess. You ought to value that differentiation even more so if you are in a couple. Maintain your independence so that you can fully appreciate the significance of your partnership. It is important that you and your partner maintain your separate identities.

I want you to know that, contrary to what you may have believed, you are not completely dried up, too old, or too chilly to be hot to trot. I know this because I want you to know that. In addition, bear in mind that regardless of where you are in your relationship, it is never too late to start over and be shameless about it. The following are some ideas that I've picked up the hard way that can assist you start ramping up the lust in your bedroom so that you may fall in love with your honey all over again:

Take care of any open wounds: Your lack of interest in having sexual encounters may be the result of physical, psychological, or profoundly emotional scars that were caused by a traumatic event, disease, or abuse. If this describes you, I strongly encourage you to investigate the possibility of receiving a refund.

support from your primary care physician, a licensed therapist, or a trained and accredited life coach. Find someone you can trust who will guide you through the process of conquering the challenges that are specific to you.

Take care of your body and work on developing a confident attitude about your curves. Own up to it. It is crucial to love and accept your body if you want to be able to feel comfortable enough to share yourself with your beloved, regardless of the size and shape of your body. I've recently made an effort to reacquaint myself with parts of my body that, due to their imperfections, I had long since given up on using. I've been touching my legs, stomach, and other parts of my body that are still warm.

during the previous year have gained weight and are not quite where I want them to be in terms of their appearance. You will have a wonderful experience if you give to and touch yourself. Test it out. Get some massage oil and apply lotion all over your body, and then make it a point to focus your attention on cultivating a closer relationship with yourself. Consider the implications of that for a moment. Where exactly have you been lacking affection in your body?

Sending yourself love is a wonderful technique to help you remember that you are wonderful exactly as you are. Then, give love and positive energy to your body while thinking positive, affirming thoughts. My appetite is dropping, and the contour of my body is effortlessly and naturally shifting as a result of the consistent practice of this activity, which I have been doing. The act of sending you additional love will also help you feel better about yourself, which is the ideal prerequisite for an evening filled with passion and enjoyment.

I was unable to rummage around and reinterpret the thousands of memories that were stored away.

I came to the conclusion that it was unnecessary for me to. Instead, I relied on a background in programming that dated back to the 1970s to write a program, put her into the deepest trance I could, and then "read it into her processor," so to speak. Soon, Amy had a mental filter in place that utilized a double bind (see Chapter 1) system that used indirect suggestion in every instance where she felt unworthy. This system would remind her of any of the thousands of small acts of kindness she engaged in naturally every year, different ones all the time, and it would also remind her, subtly, in the back of her mind, that only worthy people do these things.

She received the affirmation that "good people do these things, therefore you must be a good and worthy person" each time that her subconscious recalled an act of kindness that she had performed for another person, dating all the way back to her childhood (because our minds are constantly cycling through our memories).

I did not rephrase her requirement to take in food. I didn't do anything to improve her self-image by using positive affirmations; instead, I used indirect tactics to achieve my goal of preventing her from bringing herself down to the low level she believed she deserved to be at by shifting her perception of where that level was. I achieved this by changing the level at which she believed she deserved to be.

I was able to give her a lifelong history of small emotional boosts by creating a self-reinforcing set of emotional memories that attached themselves to her actual memories of situations and made her feel better about herself in the process. If you will, I padded her emotional history with a general feeling of self-worth without ever changing any of the memories she had of her actual life events. This allowed me to give her a lifelong history of little emotional boosts over the course of her entire life.

The binge eating ceased within a few days, and within a few weeks she was frequently engaging in walking and then running.

Within one year and eighteen months, she had regained her health, and although she had to undergo a couple of minor skin reduction surgeries to get back into shape, she was content with her life.

All of this occurred as a result of three hypnotic sessions that lasted around one hour each and took place on the same day. These sessions were aimed to create and then reinforce a Relyfe program that was intended to operate for the rest of her life.

When a person is under the influence of hypnosis, you are able to access their memories and either look at them or talk about them. alter them, and even implant them if necessary. If the person's memories are causing them issues, then they can be altered, or even better, their perspective can be altered, in order to make permanent improvements to the quality of their life.

Memory is not a factually accurate remembrance of actual events that took place in chronological order [1]. Not only does it have an influence on itself, but it also has an effect on the experiences -

and consequently the memories - of each time that it is recalled, whether consciously or unconsciously. It is chaotic and fluid, and one memory can be recalled over and over in a person's life without his or her conscious awareness.

It is simply difficult for the hypnotist to identify each and every memory that has to be addressed when confronting a problem. This is due to the fact that it is impossible to identify each and every time a life experience was later recalled and, as a result, impacted by that memory. This is the primary reason why undesirable characteristics, such as trauma, fear, anger, and so on, have a tendency to reassert themselves in a person even after an incident has been transformed in the person's memory, even after the core trauma has been discovered and dealt with. It is possible that the reason so many non-chemical addictions, in addition to some of the chemical addictions, are so difficult to overcome is due to the fact that the urge that drives the addict has been reinforced in so many situations that have been imprinted in her memories.

Sexual adultery

The teaching of the Bible with regard to adultery is quite clear. Adultery is a risky business that can lead to disastrous consequences; the dangers of this endeavor are outlined in Proverbs 5:1-11. After committing adultery with Bathsheba, King David pleaded with God for forgiveness, saying in Psalm 51:11, "Do not cast me from Your presence and do not take Your Holy Spirit from me." God did not forgive him.

Cheating causes a breach of trust in the relationship. You no longer have the same understanding of the relationship that you once did, and there is no guarantee that it will ever be the same again. It is excruciatingly distressing to consider the possibility that the person you love could entertain and carry out the idea of enjoying the same level of closeness with someone else as they do with you. An affair is a package deal that includes lies, deceit, betrayal, and broken feelings. You have a lot of questions, one of which being whether or not the love that they have pretended to have for you is genuine. Is it because of you that they choose to travel down this road?

In the book of Proverbs, verse 15 tells us to "Drink water from your own cistern," and verse 18 tells us to "Rejoice with the wife of your youth." Why, then, do people engage in dishonest behavior? Why do they act the way they do?

Why?

A person may cheat on their partner in a romantic relationship for a variety of reasons, and while this is sometimes the case, it is not necessarily reflective of or caused by the relationship that they are in.

Concern about Making a Commitment

Cheating can occur when a person is afraid of committing to their partner and as a result, they choose to damage their relationship by having an affair.

Issues Relating to One's Own Sense of Worth

A person who has low self-esteem or a negative self-image may seek the attention of others and, as a result, embark into an affair in which they can receive the interest they so desperately need.

Poor Capacity for Communication

A person who is unhappy with the tension in their relationship and their inability to communicate properly may resort to cheating in order to satisfy their emotional demands in another environment.

Void of Emotional Content

If a couple has two different love languages and they are not speaking in the appropriate love language for one other, then one of the partners in the relationship may feel unloved and turn to infidelity as a result.

Sexual Activities That Become Addictive

A person may participate in sexual practices that involve some level of risk in order to gratify their wants or to exert control over a circumstance that could be harmful to them. During one session of counseling, it was revealed that immediately after engaging in sexual activity, the man would exit the room and browse pornographic media. The absence of sexual activity was not the problem at hand; rather, the husband needed to address the behaviors that were uniquely his own.

How To Get Your Exciting Texts Started In A Snappy Manner

"I can't wait to see you tonight," stated the man. My opinion is that it would be wonderful to let loose and have some fun.

Because I'm in the mood to have fun, when I get home you should already be in your underwear, even if you're not.

"Baby, I couldn't be more horny if I tried. In your opinion, what kind of attire should I wear to my date later tonight?I had the sexiest dream about us last night, and it inspired me for our date night next weekend ;)" I promise that I have a steamy surprise in store for you tonight.

Due to the fact that I can't stop thinking about the date that you and I had the night before, I'm having trouble concentrating at work today.

I have literally just stepped out of the shower... would you like to see? - (Preparing a steamy shot) If you don't reside with your significant other, what are you planning on doing later tonight? Do you mind if I stop by to give you a quick blow or a go down on you? Right this second, I have a ravenous appetite for either your cock or your pussy in my mouth.

- (Having a picture of a sensual scene ready) "Would you like to look at a picture that I just snapped for you? I'm patting myself on the back right now while reflecting on what we did the night before.Mm... the events of last night are still causing me quite a bit of discomfort. Whether you're with a woman or a man, you certainly know how to have a good time.

Do you wish to come up with your very own one-of-a-kind tease texts? A good rule of thumb is to recall a single instance from your most recent trip that made you really excited, then explain it and let them know it's on your mind. For example, "I'm currently contemplating you nonstop while I'm sitting at the counter in my kitchen." I can't wait to feel your skin on mine once more. [Put in the emojis for an eggplant, a peach, a raindrop, and a jaw-dropped expression here]

Are you willing to work on making it better? Send them an SMS either before or after you masturbate. It is recommended that you only share this message with very close friends or intimate partners who you see on a regular basis.

As you'll see, it absolutely belongs in the "Intermediate" and "Advanced" categories, but it's a huge turn on and fosters a greater feeling of sexual openness.

Examples include "I've been thinking about you riding me, for sure."

"I worked myself up into a frenzy just thinking about it. I'm going to act on my own initiative.

Dirty Talk for Beginners, Intermediates, and Advanced

If you've been following my writing for some time, you may be aware that I tend to favor pretty polarized sex. Which means that a lot of my nasty conversations involve the dominant/submissive roles being played out.

Strategies For Creating Sexual Tension Via Text Message With A Woman

There are a variety of strategies that can be utilized to heighten the sexual tension between two people. However, there is something that is significantly more important than the words you choose or the manner in which you express them. That something is the attitude that you take toward the entire circumstance. When you're trying to chat to a lady in person or text her and you don't know how to initiate the conversation, flirting can be difficult. This is especially true if you're not sure how to initiate the conversation.

Creating sexual tension with a woman may be accomplished in a number of different ways. One of these ways is by flirting with her. It is necessary to have the ability to tease her and make her feel as though she needs to impress you in order to succeed. The sexual tension between the two of you can increase thanks to flirting, and it can also let her know that you find her attractive and want her. The fact that you are willing to flirt with a woman who has piqued your attention might also demonstrate to her that you have a high level of self-assurance in both your abilities and in yourself.

It is essential to keep in mind that flirting with someone via text is not the same as flirting with them in person. There are no visual indicators to guide you through a conversation with a woman that takes place solely through text. It is not the same as flirting in person since there are no hand signals or facial expressions to interpret, and it is also very different from flirting online because you do not have to observe the other person to figure out what makes her squirm or gives her chills.

What exactly is sexual tension, though?

Sexual tension is an emotional response that occurs between two people who are extremely attracted to one another and are in close proximity to one another. It generates a sense of suspense and excitement, as you yearn for the other person intensely but are unsure whether they feel the same way about you as you do about them. Teasing and flirting with someone, whether it be through text or in person, can help to amp up the sexual tension between the two of you.

The majority of people appreciate the sexual tension that might arise between them, particularly if they are attracted to one another and have similar values. When someone flirts with them, the majority of people feel good about themselves and their capacity to attract a spouse because they want to believe that they are capable of attracting someone that they like.

I have provided a list of some of the flirting techniques that you can use to excite a girl's hormones even when the two of you are not physically present together.

1. Teases of a Joking Nature

Teases are great fun for women. It demonstrates to them not only that you are interested in them, but also that you are witty and have a wonderful sense of humor, which is an even more compelling message to send. To generate sexual tension with a woman, one of the most effective methods to use flirting is to find out how much she enjoys being teased, and once you know this, you will have discovered one of the finest ways to use flirting.

You can make fun of her by calling her an embarrassing nickname. The use of a nickname for her will demonstrate to her that you are interested in developing a closer relationship with her and that you want to be around her. When someone goes to the effort of giving you a cute nickname, it's a clear indication that they care about you. You can also tease her by reminding her of anything she has done or said in the past and laughing at her expense.

A woman wants to be with a man who can make them laugh, and once she learns that you're able to make her laugh at herself, she'll know that you're interested in being with her as well. A woman wants to be with a man who can make them laugh because they want to be with a man who can make them laugh. After a stressful day at work or dealing with just about anything else that comes up during the day, a woman needs time to relax and focus on herself.

2. Exhibit the Sinful Side of Yourself

Women are drawn to males who have an element of the bad boy about them. You can have a naughty side while still being the perfect gentleman, but the manner in which you show her your naughty side is what will make her fall in love with you. She will fall in love with you because of how you show her your naughty side. You're going to have to pull out all the stops if you want to convince her that the naughty side of you isn't nearly as horrible as it seems on the surface.

It is appropriate to let her know that you are interested in her physically; nevertheless, this does not mean that you should give her images of your private parts. That is just too strenuous. You have to be imaginative while keeping your etiquette at the same level. Asking her in jest what she's wearing is a good idea. Send her an image of a sensual product, such as undergarments or cologne, and tell her that you've been considering purchasing it for her as a gift for a while now.

Not only will this demonstrate to her the kind of person she is interacting with, but it will also indicate that you are interested in what it is about her that makes her who she is. When playing naughty, you need to take things slowly or she might get the impression that it's too much for her. But teasing is one thing that will never lose its place in a woman's heart as one of the finest methods to use flirting to create sexual tension with a woman. Teasing is one of the best ways to use flirting to make a woman feel sexually attracted to you.

3. Put Yourself in Danger

Even though you're texting her, that doesn't mean she can't learn more about you and your life in the process. You decide how much information you want her to have about your life and what your goals are for the future. She will only know as much as you tell her. If the only thing a woman knows about you is that you are successful and wealthy, then she will begin to feel as though she is not enough if you continue to treat her in this manner.

You need to be able to test her limits and demonstrate to her that you still want to be with her even though she does not have all the answers to the big questions in her life, such as who she is and where her life is going. You need to create an air of mystery around yourself and demonstrate to her how much you take pleasure in the simple pleasures of life, such as sharing a meal in front of the fireplace or watching the sun go down together.

It is not necessary for you to reassure her that you would provide her with all that money can buy. The more time she spends with you, the more likely it is that she will start to fall in love with you due to your own distinct personality and all of the beautiful qualities that you possess that set you apart from every other man in the world.

As a result of the tension that has built up between the two of you, it is time to take the conversation that you have been having via text messages to the next level. Keep in mind that every woman is unique and may have a different reaction to what you say or do depending on her personality. It is essential to pay attention to the reactions that a woman gives since what is successful for one woman may not be successful for another.

A way out

If you want to have a conversation about sexual issues in your relationship with your spouse, the most uncomfortable position to be in is when you are nude and exposed. Find a place where you won't be interrupted, where you can be alone, and where you can have some privacy.

You should try your utmost to avoid feeling guilty while still expressing your sensitivity. It is crucial to talk about your concerns, but rather than stating "you" make "me" worried, frame the conversation within the framework of your relationship. Anxiety is to fault for this situation.

If your partner does not know what the cause of the problem is but acknowledges that there is a problem, propose that your doctor perform a physical assessment on your partner. Low libido is frequently the result of an undetected medical problem (such as low testosterone, high blood pressure, hypothyroidism, or diabetes), or it can be a side effect of some medications (such as antidepressants, birth control pills, and some medications for the prostate).

You shouldn't take the situation personally and should instead hold yourself accountable if your partner avoids talking about the problem or shuts the door on the conversation altogether. In the end, this is not what your ex-partner or ex-partner has left behind for you. They must both contribute to the problem by having certain characteristics. You can shed light on the problem and use the process to improve the connection with your partner by guiding them through couples therapy and offering it to them when it's necessary.

Work together to find a solution to the issue if your partner has identified a problem, such as stress at work or chronic exhaustion, for example. Keep an eye out for any subsequent alterations, and get medical help if necessary. Don't be afraid to provide treatment to the patient.

This therapy can be helpful in identifying difficulties of mental health conditions like depression or anxiety, as well as providing methods for managing stress. As you look for long-term solutions, you should make sure that you stress the significance of both emotional and physical closeness to one another.

It is essential to keep in mind that addressing issues in a relationship, whether they are of a sexual, financial, or emotional nature, is a process and not a one-time occurrence. Take things slowly, practice patience, and consult a therapist if necessary to keep your self-esteem and keep your confidence up.

www.ingramcontent.com/pod-product-compliance
Lightning Source LLC
Chambersburg PA
CBHW050243120526
44590CB00016B/2190